CONSERVATION AREAS

Jack and Meg Gillett

With contributions by Richard and Louise Spilsbury

WAYLAND

Contents

About this book

Our planet and all the living things on it are under threat from people. We are harming many habitats and ecosystems through mining, drilling, fishing and other activities in order to obtain the resources demanded by our growing population. We are mostly causing damaging pollution and global warming through using energy to power vehicles and generate electricity.

Conservation is the protection of wild places and living things. It is vital to protect global biodiversity to ensure species survive into the future, not least because some may become useful or valuable, for example to improve human health. It is impossible to conserve all places on Earth, but there are many conservation areas, some protecting large regions and others just a few rare species.

This book looks at the location and variety of conservation areas, the wildlife and places they seek to protect, and the challenges to and successes of the conservation measures put in place to protect them. It also locates areas that are threatened or will be in the near future and that are in need of conservation measures.

Map shows the location of the endangered areas discussed

Globe shows the location of the map region

Key explains the symbols used in the map

Pictures highlight features discussed or located on the map

Fun research activity

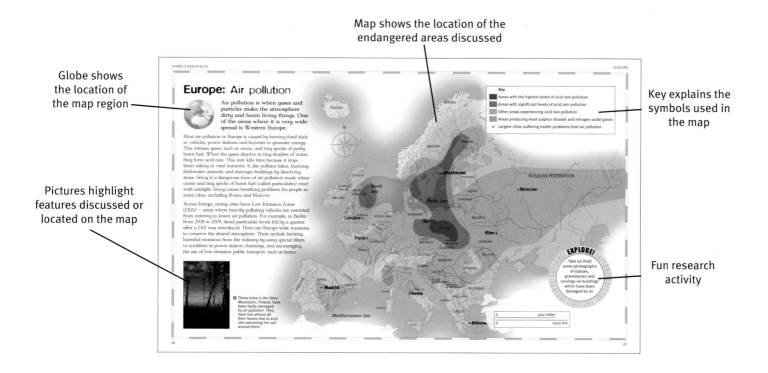

British Isles: Landscape conservation

Despite the relatively small size of the British Isles, they have a great variety of landscapes. There are fields and hedges, hills and mountains, moorland and woodland, rivers and long stretches of coastline.

In the past, large areas of countryside were gradually lost to new buildings, industries and farming developments. Since 1951, 15 large areas of countryside have been designated National Parks, including Dartmoor National Park and the Yorkshire Dales. These are areas of beautiful countryside and wildlife that are conserved (protected) by planning controls so they cannot be spoilt. They are owned and cared for by a mix of private landowners, such as farmers, organisations, such as the National Trust, and National Park Authorities.

There are also about 50 Areas of Outstanding Natural Beauty (AONBs) in the British Isles. These are special or beautiful landscapes that are smaller than national parks, but which still need protecting. Sites of Special Scientific Interest (SSSIs) are even smaller protected habitats, such as wetlands, meadows, or woodland, for example Wytham Woods in Oxfordshire. Most of them are internationally important because of the endangered wildlife living there. There are over 4,000 Sites of Special Scientific Interest (SSSIs) in England alone!

EXPLORE!

Hedges are one of nature's richest wildlife habitats. Use http://hedgelink.org.uk/index.php?id=26 to list five different insects, birds and small mammals that thrive in hedges in the British Isles.

⬆ The Lake District is the most famous of all Britain's National Parks. Its mountains have a variety of shapes because they are made of different types of rock which were eroded by glaciers during the Ice Age.

⬆ Wytham Woods by Oxford became one of the first SSSIs in 1950 and is one of the world's most studied habitats. Observing the woods over a long time has helped scientists understand how different plants might be affected by global warming, for example.

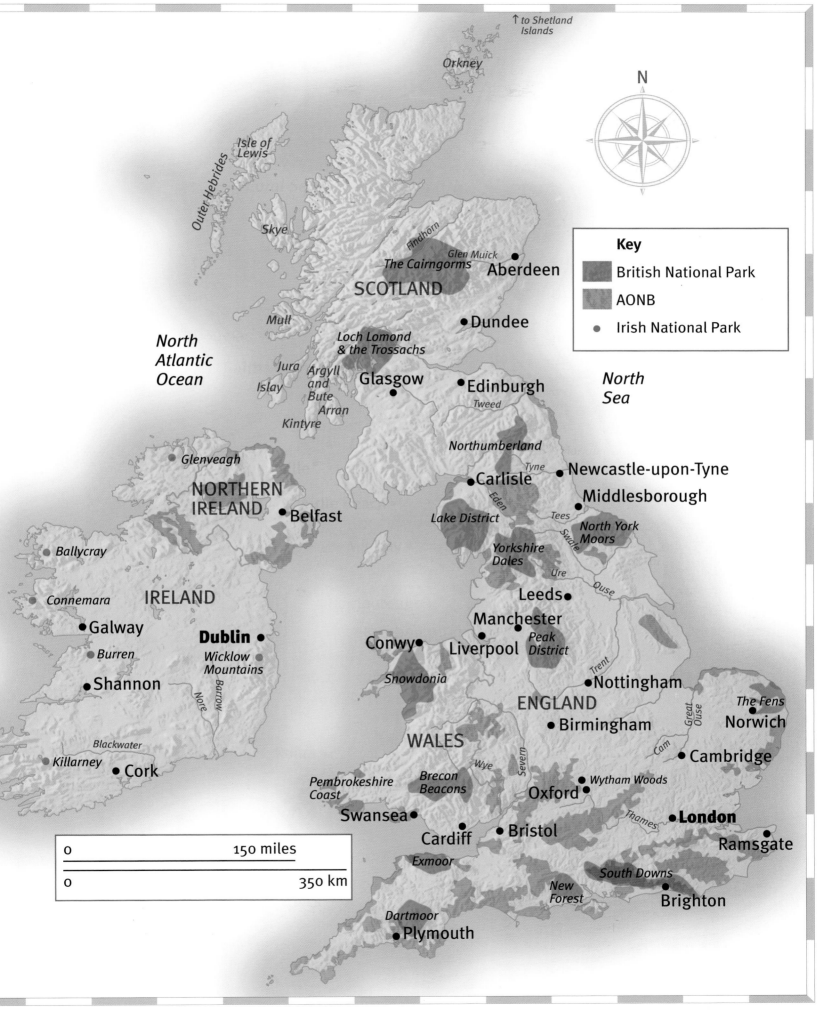

↑ to Shetland Islands

Orkney

Isle of Lewis

Outer Hebrides

Skye

Findhorn

Glen Muick

The Cairngorms

● Aberdeen

SCOTLAND

Mull

● Dundee

North Atlantic Ocean

Jura

Argyll and Bute

Islay

Arran

Kintyre

Loch Lomond & the Trossachs

Glasgow ●

● Edinburgh

Tweed

North Sea

Key

British National Park

AONB

● Irish National Park

Glenveagh ●

Northumberland

NORTHERN IRELAND

● Carlisle

Tyne

● Newcastle-upon-Tyne

● Belfast

Eden

Middlesborough

Lake District

Tees

North York Moors

Ballycray ●

Yorkshire Dales

Swale

Ure

Connemara ●

IRELAND

Ouse

● Leeds

● Galway

Manchester ●

Burren ●

Dublin ●

Conwy ●

Liverpool ●

Peak District

Wicklow Mountains ●

● Shannon

Snowdonia

Trent

● Nottingham

Barrow

Nore

ENGLAND

● Birmingham

The Fens

WALES

Great Ouse

Blackwater

Wye

Severn

Cam

● Norwich

Killarney ●

● Cork

Brecon Beacons

Wytham Woods ●

● Cambridge

Pembrokeshire Coast

Oxford ●

Swansea ●

Thames

● **London**

Cardiff ●

● Bristol

Exmoor

South Downs

● Ramsgate

New Forest

Dartmoor

● Brighton

● Plymouth

0	150 miles
0	350 km

N

South America:
Sustainable forestry

Trees are vital to life on Earth because they absorb carbon dioxide from the air and replace it with oxygen. But trees are being cut down, especially in tropical rainforests.

Warm, humid tropical rainforest is home to almost 70 per cent of all species. Much is located in South America, but under threat because trees are being felled faster than they are being replanted. Deforestation here is driven by demand for timber and wood products, including plywood and paper. The cleared land is also used to raise cattle for beef and as a source for valuable oil. These activities are important to the economic development of less developed countries such as Brazil because they generate income to invest in new roads, hospitals and other infrastructure.

South American governments completely protect some areas of forest, such as the Juruena National Park in Brazil, to stop deforestation. But as the rainforest is so enormous and economically important, they also manage areas of forest sustainably. Sustainable forestry controls deforestation and replants land with native species to maintain biodiversity and forest size. It conserves the shared forest resource into the future for people and wildlife. In Bolivia, the deforestation rate is actually slower in sustainably managed forest than in protected areas.

⬆ The Iguazú falls are shared by the Iguazú National Park (Argentina) and Iguacu National Park (Brazil). These parks are UNESCO World Heritage sites.

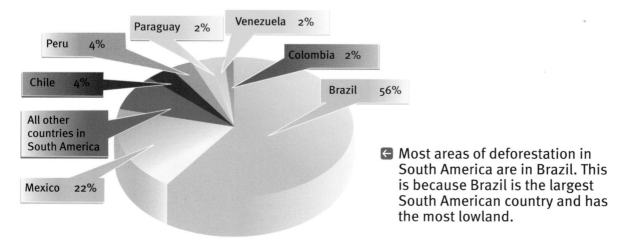

Peru 4%

Paraguay 2%

Venezuela 2%

Colombia 2%

Chile 4%

Brazil 56%

All other countries in South America

Mexico 22%

⬅ Most areas of deforestation in South America are in Brazil. This is because Brazil is the largest South American country and has the most lowland.

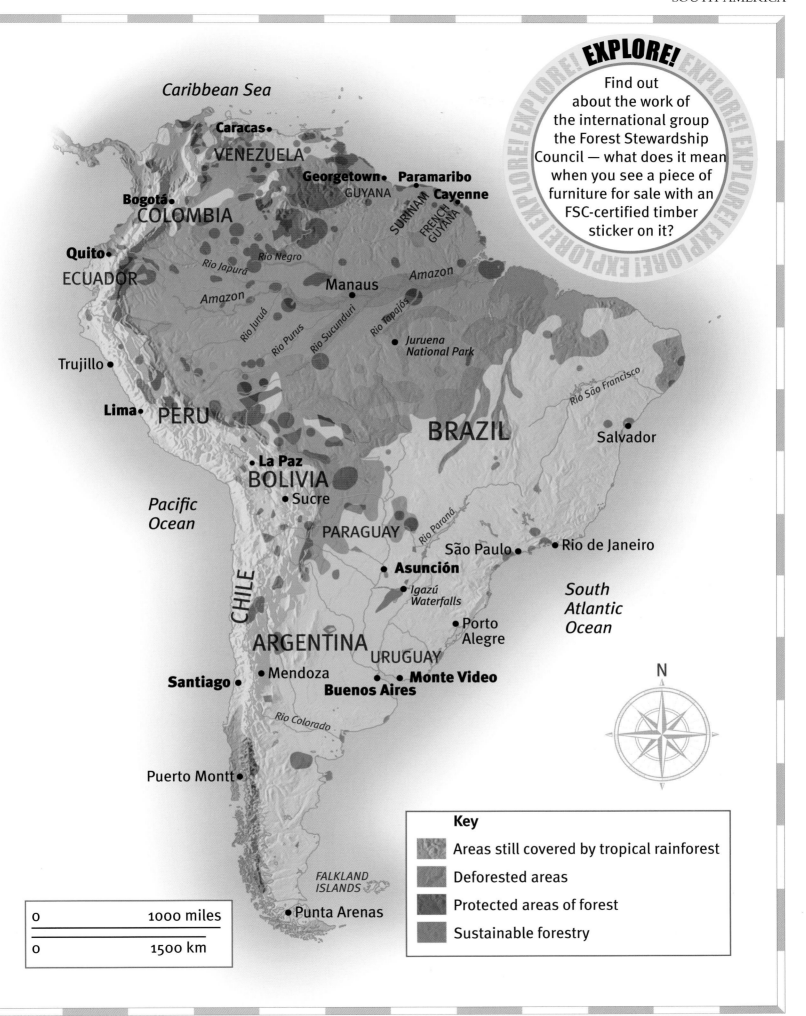

Caribbean Sea

Caracas•
VENEZUELA
Georgetown• Paramaribo
GUYANA
Cayenne
SURINAM
FRENCH GUYANA
Bogotá•
COLOMBIA
Rio Negro
Quito•
Rio Japurá
ECUADOR
Amazon
Manaus
Amazon
Rio Juruá
Rio Purus
Rio Sucunduri
Rio Tapajós
Trujillo •
Juruena National Park
Lima• PERU
Rio São Francisco
BRAZIL
Salvador
• La Paz
BOLIVIA
• Sucre
Pacific Ocean
Rio Paraná
PARAGUAY
São Paulo• • Rio de Janeiro
• Asunción
South Atlantic Ocean
Igazú Waterfalls
CHILE
• Porto Alegre
ARGENTINA
URUGUAY
• Mendoza
Santiago • • Monte Video
Buenos Aires
Rio Colorado

N

Puerto Montt•

FALKLAND ISLANDS

Key	
	Areas still covered by tropical rainforest
	Deforested areas
	Protected areas of forest
	Sustainable forestry

0   1000 miles

0   1500 km

• Punta Arenas

Western USA: Saving the soil

Western USA has large areas of desert, including the Mojave and Sonoran, and dry land. They are caused by being in the rainshadow of the mountain ranges including the Sierra Nevada.

Many of the drier areas in western USA are in danger of desertification. This is when land dries out or becomes damaged, so the soil crumbles to dust. Wind-blown dust chokes water channels and blows onto settlements and farmland. Scientists predict that the remaining dry grasslands of the western USA are threatened by desertification because of higher temperatures. This is a result of global warming and droughts caused by changing weather patterns.

One of the worst cases of desertification in history happened in the Dust Bowl of central USA in the 1930s. Soil turned to giant dust clouds because of land damage through ploughing and several years of drought. Thousands of farming families had to leave the area. Farming in the region recovered when it started raining again, but it relies on irrigation from underground water supplies that are reducing every year.

EXPLORE!

The Atacama Desert can't spread outwards to the west or the east. Discover why not.

In southwest USA people are trying to prevent desertification in different ways. For example, farmers plant trees or build fences to trap blown soil. They improve the soil condition by planting deep-rooted crops and leaving crop remains in fields after harvest, so roots hold onto soil.

⬅ US farmers use a relatively new technique called no-till when planting new seed. Instead of ploughing the soil, machines create a thin slit for the seed, which means the top soil remains undisturbed and covered by crop remains. This protects soil from erosion.

CANADA

N

Seattle
Washington

Montana

North Dakota

Lake Superior

The Great Lakes

Oregon

Idaho

Minnesota

Michigan

Lake Huron

Wisconsin

Mississippi River

South Dakota

Missouri River

Wyoming

Nevada

California

Sacramento
San Francisco

Sierra Nevada

Utah

Denver

Platte River

Nebraska

Iowa

Lake Michigan

Chicago

Lake Erie

USA

Illinois

Indiana

Kansas City

St. Louis

Kentucky

Las Vegas

Colorado

Beaver River

Kansas

Missouri

Death Valley
(highest temperature 57°C)

Painted Desert

Oklahoma

Arkansas

Tennessee

Los Angeles

Mojave Desert

Arizona

Canadian River

Memphis

Sonoran Desert

Phoenix

New Mexico

Colorado River

Arkansas River

Alabama

Dallas

Louisiana

Mississippi

MEXICO

Texas

Austin

New Orleans

San Antonio

Gulf of Mexico

| 0 | 500 miles |
| 0 | 1000 km |

Key

Hot desert areas

Areas of greatest risk of desertification

Areas of significant risk of desertification

Other areas at risk of desertification

Area which became known as the Dust Bowl after the soil erosion of the early 1930s

Unusually hot, dry years lead to drought.

Without water, crops and grass wither and die.

Without plant cover, the topsoil is exposed and there are no roots to bind it together.

Bare soil turns to dust if walked on by herds of buffalo or cattle.

Strong winds lift the dusty soil and blow it away. This is called erosion.

⬆ This diagram shows how soil erosion takes place.

East Africa: Wildlife conservation

East Africa is home to some of the greatest concentrations of large mammals on Earth. Its wildlife is especially threatened by poaching – illegal hunting – supplying the illegal black market trade.

Elephants and rhinos are shot or killed in traps by poachers, mostly to hack off their tusks or horns. The ivory that forms elephant tusks is used to make decorative objects. Rhino horns are used in traditional medicines in China and in Africa, and as ceremonial dagger handles in countries including Yemen. Other wild animals, including giraffe, rare antelopes and even chimpanzees, are poached for bushmeat. Many countries and Internet sites ban the sale of poached goods, but the black market thrives because of the value of this trade. For example, a pair of tusks can fetch almost US$100,000.

Africa has around 300 National Parks and hundreds of smaller reserves where armed rangers try to keep poachers out. However, this is difficult when few rangers protect large areas. For example, the Kenyan Wildlife Service has 1500 rangers in 22 National Parks (not all of which are large enough to show on the map). One of them is Tsavo, which covers a total area twice the size of Wales. East African conservation areas also protect habitats from destruction by farmers and mining companies.

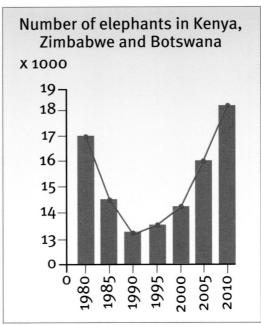

Number of elephants in Kenya, Zimbabwe and Botswana

X 1000

⭡ This line graph shows how the elephant population in three African countries changed between 1980 and 2010. The recent increase is due to the protection given by National Parks and game reserves.

⭡ Zebras by a lake in the Serengeti National Park in Tanzania.

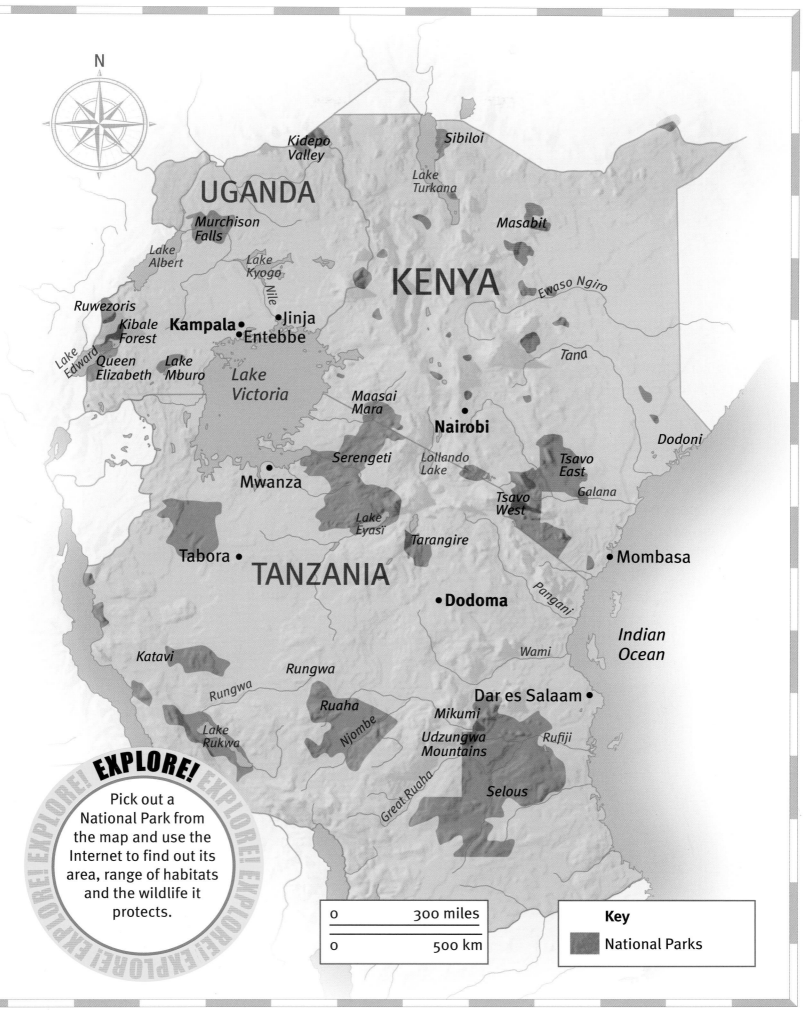

N

Kidepo
Valley

Sibiloi

UGANDA

Lake
Turkana

Murchison
Falls

Masabit

Lake
Albert

Lake
Kyogo

KENYA

Nile

Ruwezoris

Ewaso Ngiro

Kibale
Forest

Kampala • •Jinja
•Entebbe

Lake
Edward

Queen
Elizabeth

Lake
Mburo

Lake
Victoria

Tana

Maasai
Mara

Nairobi

Dodoni

Serengeti

Lollando
Lake

Tsavo
East

•Mwanza

Galana

Lake
Eyasi

Tsavo
West

Tarangire

TANZANIA

Tabora •

•Mombasa

•**Dodoma**

Pangani

Indian
Ocean

Wami

Katavi

Rungwa

Rungwa

Dar es Salaam •

Ruaha

Mikumi

Lake
Rukwa

Njombe

Udzungwa
Mountains

Rufiji

Great Ruaha

Selous

EXPLORE!

Pick out a
National Park from
the map and use the
Internet to find out its
area, range of habitats
and the wildlife it
protects.

0		300 miles
0		500 km

Key

National Parks

Asia: Species conservation

Asia's human population is the fastest-growing on the planet and this puts great pressure on wildlife habitats. As a result, its native tigers and apes, such as orang-utan, are among the 'top 10' of endangered species.

Habitat loss is one of the largest threats to species around the world. This can happen for many reasons, but all are due to growth of human population, such as the expansion of cities and deforestation for timber or farmland. For example, the giant panda, which eats only bamboo, became endangered when bamboo forests were cleared to grow more crops for China's rising population.

Species that are globally in danger are put on the IUCN Red List of Threatened Species. This identifies species requiring conservation in order to avoid the risk of extinction. Many of Asia's species are on the list, including orang-utan in Indonesia and Malaysia, and tigers throughout the region. Today there are fewer than 3,000 tigers in Asia. This is because of poaching for body parts, used in traditional medicines, and because the forest habitats they live and hunt in have been extensively cut down over the last century. Some tigers are protected in conservation areas, including 39 Project Tiger reserves in India, but in many parts of Asia tigers have little protection.

⬅ A young orang-utan in Borneo's Sepilok Forest Reserve.

EXPLORE!
Make a list of 10 critically endangered Asian species from the Red List by visiting the website www. iucnredlist.org .

N

RUSSIA

KAZAKHSTAN

•Ulan Bator

MONGOLIA

•Urumqi

KYRGYZSTAN

TAJIKISTAN

•Beijing •

JAPAN

NORTH KOREA

SOUTH KOREA

•Jinan

CHINA

•Lanzhou

•Shanghai

PAKISTAN

•Islamabad

•Xi'an
•Wuhan

Nepal

•Chongqing

•Fuzhou

TAIWAN

Delhi •

INDIA

•Guiyang

Pacific
Ocean

BANGLADESH

•Hong Kong

•Nanning

BURMA

Hainan

LAOS

Bay of
Bengal

THAILAND

•Manila

PHILIPPINES

VIETNAM

Bangkok

Phnom Penh•

•Ho Chi Minh

CAMBODIA

Sepilok Forest
Reserve

BRUNEI

MALAYSIA

Borneo

Celebes

•Kuala Lumpur
•Singapore

INDONESIA

Key

Tiger habitats 100 years ago

Tiger habitats at present

India's tiger reserves

•Jakarta

0	1000 miles
0	1000 km

Europe: Wetland conservation

Wetlands are ecosystems including bogs and swamps where the soil is saturated with water for all or most of the year. They are very important ecosystems as they hold water and control flooding.

Europe's wetlands are under threat. Since 1900, around 60 per cent of the original area of Europe's wetlands has disappeared. This is a result of draining to create farmland, build new homes on, and extract freshwater for the growing population. Smaller wetlands not only have fewer habitats for wildlife, but also store less freshwater that humans and other animals need. Recreational use, such as boating and fishing, disturbs water birds and other wetland animals, especially during their breeding seasons. This means that their numbers are falling. Wetlands are also polluted by agricultural and industrial chemicals washed off the land. This impacts on the wildlife and water plants, too. One in three European freshwater fish species are threatened because of changes to wetlands.

Conserving existing wetlands is now a high environmental priority across Europe. Some are conserved in National Parks and reserves. For example, in Britain, the Wildfowl and Wetlands Trust runs reserves where it plants new reed-bed habitats, keeps lakes at a constant depth and makes sure the water is clean to encourage breeding water birds.

⬆ Martin Mere is one of the Wildfowl and Wetlands Trust's sites. It is also an SSSI and a favourite stopping-off point for migrating geese and swans.

⬅ The Camargue Regional Park, southern France, is one of Europe's largest wetlands. This protected area is famous for its wild horses and colourful flamingos.

PORTUGAL

Delta of the River Guadalquiver

EXPLORE!

Find out about the Ramsar Convention and its importance for wetland ecosystem conservation worldwide.

Key

Wetland reserve

Wetland

ICELAND

Arctic Ocean

N

SWEDEN

NORWAY

FINLAND

•**Stockholm**

ESTONIA

Estonia Marshes

LATVIA

Scotland

Northern Ireland

North Sea

UNITED KINGDOM

Ireland

DENMARK

Baltic Sea

LITHUANIA

RUSS. FED.

Wales

Martin Mere Wetland Centre

England

The Fens

NETHERLANDS

BELARUS

London •

BELGIUM

GERMANY

•**Berlin**

POLAND

Kiev •

Poitevin Marsh

Paris•

CZECH REPUBLIC

UKRAINE

FRANCE

SLOVAKIA

SWITZERLAND

AUSTRIA

HUNGARY

MOLDOVA

Alps

Alps

SLOVENIA

ROMANIA

Delta of the River Danube

Pyrenees

ANDORRA

The Camargue

CROATIA

SAN MARINO

BOSNIA HERZEGOVINA

SERBIA & MONTENEGRO

Black Sea

•**Madrid**

SPAIN

ITALY

Mostar Marshes

BULGARIA

Corsica

VATICAN CITY

•**Rome**

MACEDONIA

ALBANIA

Sardinia

Mediterranean Sea

GREECE

Sicily

•**Athens**

MALTA

0	500 miles
0	1000 km

New Zealand: Marine conservation

Oceans and seas cover two-thirds of our planet. They are complex ecosystems that are rich in wildlife, but increasingly endangered due to human activities.

Many marine species are endangered. Some are harmed by pollution, for example resulting from spilled oil and industrial chemicals, and ships dumping harmful rubbish in oceans. Enormous trawlers netting anything in their path can destroy whole populations of fish.

New Zealand is a pioneer in marine conservation with over 30 marine reserves. The map shows where they are located. The first ever marine reserve, around Goat Island, was created in 1975 and transformed the overfished waters into a richly biodiverse area. It is a 'no-take' reserve, which means all fishing is banned, but tourist divers are welcome to swim and look, but never kill or otherwise disturb wildlife. There are no barriers around the reserve, but conservation rangers patrol the area. In other countries marine parks, sanctuaries and reserves provide different levels of conservation. For example, fishing, dredging and other activities are allowed, but strictly controlled in US marine sanctuaries.

EXPLORE!

Find out about the species and marine landscape conserved at two different marine reserves using the interactive map at www. doc.govt.nz/conservation/ marine-and-coastal/marine-protected-areas/marine-reserves-a-z/.

Around 12 per cent of land is protected, but only under 0.5 per cent of oceans and seas are. The pressure is growing to catch more fish and find more oil under sea beds. However, more countries are conserving their waters. For example, in October 2010 the UK established the largest no-take marine protected area in the world in the Chagos Archipelago in the Indian ocean.

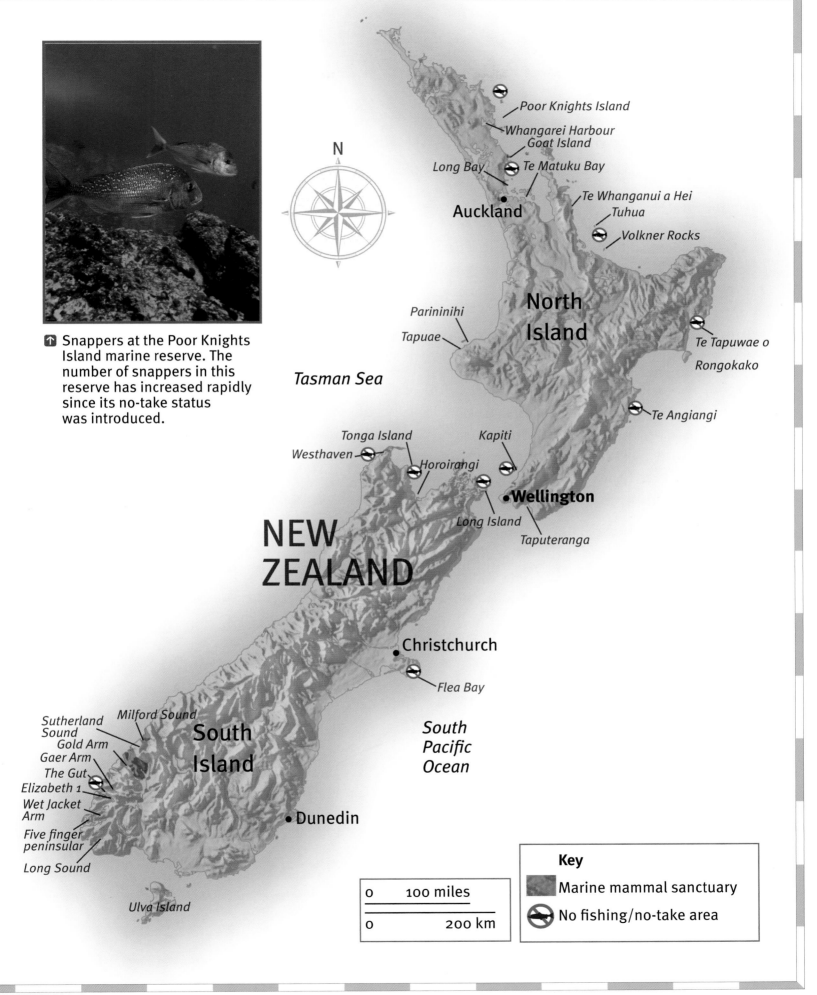

↑ Snappers at the Poor Knights Island marine reserve. The number of snappers in this reserve has increased rapidly since its no-take status was introduced.

N

Poor Knights Island

Whangarei Harbour
Goat Island

Long Bay — **Te Matuku Bay**

Te Whanganui a Hei
Tuhua

Auckland

Volkner Rocks

North Island

Parininihi

Tapuae

Te Tapuwae o Rongokako

Tasman Sea

Te Angiangi

Tonga Island   Kapiti

Westhaven — **Horoirangi**

Taputeranga

Long Island

Wellington

NEW ZEALAND

Christchurch

Flea Bay

South Pacific Ocean

South Island

Sutherland Sound   Milford Sound
Gold Arm
Gaer Arm
The Gut
Elizabeth 1
Wet Jacket Arm
Five finger peninsular
Long Sound

• Dunedin

Ulva Island

0	100 miles
0	200 km

Key

Marine mammal sanctuary

No fishing/no-take area

Antarctica: Fragile environments

Antarctica is the permanently ice-covered continent centred on the South Pole. It has the coldest, windiest climate on Earth and is surrounded by the freezing, rough Southern Ocean.

Few life forms can survive on Antarctic land other than lichens, although penguins breed there in the slightly warmer summer. However, vast numbers of microscopic phytoplankton grow in the mineral-rich waters supporting the Antarctic food web. Phytoplankton are eaten by shrimp-like animals called krill. Krill are the main food not only for fish eaten by penguins and seabirds, but also for the enormous blue, fin and sei whales.

Global warming is raising the temperature of the Southern Ocean and shrinking its sea ice. Krill numbers are falling because there are fewer phytoplankton, which flourish best under sea ice and in colder water. They are also falling because of illegal overfishing. There are fewer whales as there are fewer krill but also because of illegal whaling. This is despite the Southern Ocean Whale Sanctuary, an area where whaling is banned.

Antarctica was harmed by waste dumping from scientific stations before they were banned under the international Antarctic Treaty in 1959. (The map shows the scientific stations and which countries they belong to.) However, global demand for the abundant minerals hidden under the ice, and oil discovered deep in the South Atlantic, may threaten Antarctica in future.

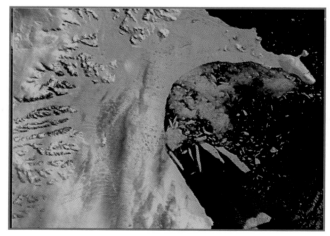

⬆ Parts of the Antarctic ice shelf are retreating further every year due to global warming. This image shows an 800-square kilometre ice shelf collapsing into the Weddell Sea.

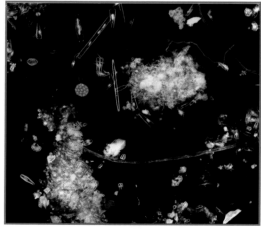

⬆ Microscopic phytoplankton are essential to the whole Antarctic food web.

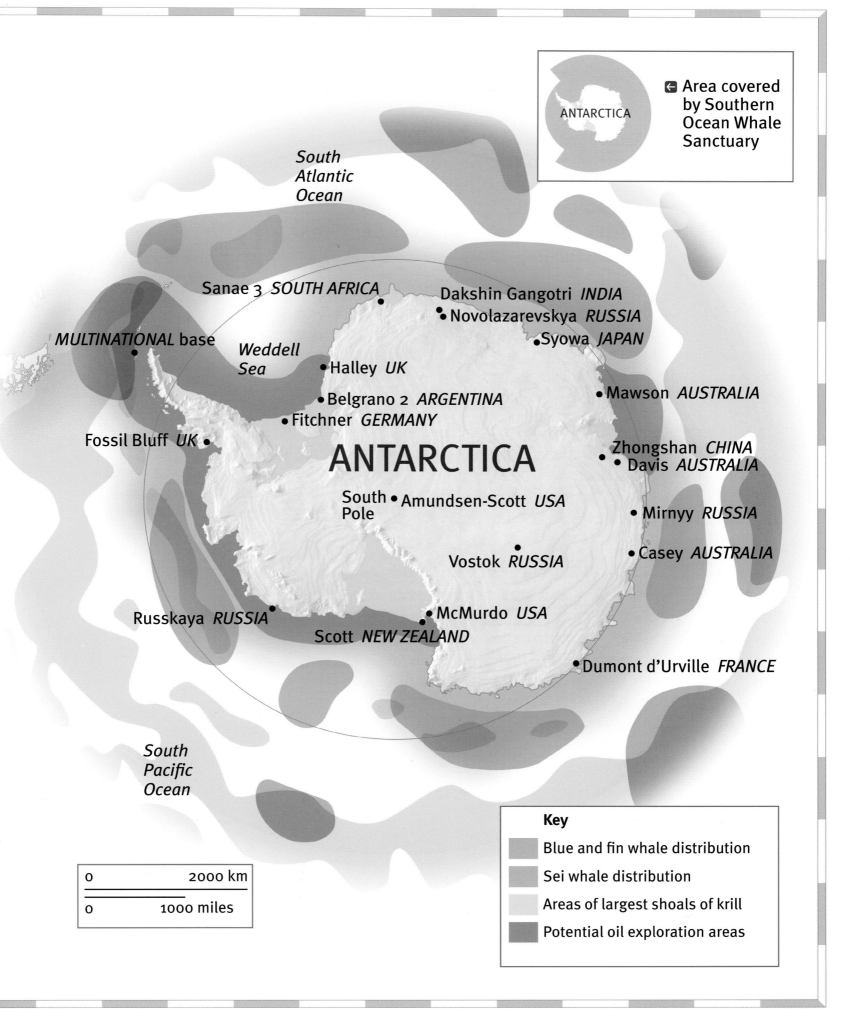

South Atlantic Ocean

Area covered by Southern Ocean Whale Sanctuary

ANTARCTICA

Sanae 3 *SOUTH AFRICA*

Dakshin Gangotri *INDIA*
Novolazarevskya *RUSSIA*
Syowa *JAPAN*

MULTINATIONAL base

Weddell Sea

Halley *UK*

Mawson *AUSTRALIA*

Belgrano 2 *ARGENTINA*
Fitchner *GERMANY*

Fossil Bluff *UK*

ANTARCTICA

Zhongshan *CHINA*
Davis *AUSTRALIA*

South Pole • Amundsen-Scott *USA*

Mirnyy *RUSSIA*

Vostok *RUSSIA*

Casey *AUSTRALIA*

Russkaya *RUSSIA*

McMurdo *USA*
Scott *NEW ZEALAND*

Dumont d'Urville *FRANCE*

South Pacific Ocean

Key

Blue and fin whale distribution

Sei whale distribution

Areas of largest shoals of krill

Potential oil exploration areas

0	2000 km
0	1000 miles

Australia: Coral reefs

Coral reefs are often called 'the rainforests of the sea' because they are the habitat for an extraordinary range of wildlife. The 2,300 km-long Great Barrier Reef in Australia is the world's largest reef system.

Reefs are formed by tiny marine animals, called coral polyps, that live in big colonies. Polyps secrete protective mineral skeletons around their bodies, so rock-like reefs gradually form over many years. Polyps survive because tiny algae inside their bodies make food using sunlight. Coral needs warm, clear water with enough minerals to make skeletons.

One in ten reefs globally have been destroyed by people, such as fishermen using dynamite to catch fish. Reefs are damaged when tourists walk on coral and break off pieces as souvenirs. Corals are sensitive to global warming. For example, coral dies and turns white (bleaches) in warmer water because algae in polyps die.

EXPLORE!
Visit www.reefed.edu.au/home/explorer/animals/marine_invertebrates/echinoderms/crown_of_thorns to investigate the major natural threat to corals making up the Great Barrier Reef.

The Great Barrier Reef is a UNESCO World Heritage area. This recognizes the natural, cultural and economic importance of the reef and encourages tourism. There is also a larger Marine Park run by the Australian government to conserve the reef. Park maps are colour zoned — no-one can enter pink zones without official permission, but tourists can boat and dive in light-blue zones.

⬆ When corals die, a whole habitat disappears with them. Areas of dead coral in the Great Barrier Reef are deserted of marine wildlife.

⬆ Conservation measures have been very successful in recovering some of the badly affected areas of the Great Barrier Reef.

Warrior Reefs

Murray Islands

Moa Island

• Rocky Point

Key

— Boundary of the Great Barrier Reef Marine Park

— Boundary of the World Heritage site (which includes all the islands in the Great Barrier Reef)

Coral Sea

Osprey Reef

N

Cairns Reef

Port Douglas •

Arlington Reef

Cairns •

• Karumba

Holmes Reef

Flinders Reef

Lihou Reef

Pacific Ocean

Slashers Reefs

Marion Reef

Hook Reef

Townsville •

Airlie Beach •

• Richmond

Swain Reefs

Mackay •

Saumarez Reef

AUSTRALIA

Marlborough •

Blackall •

Rockhampton •

Queensland

Quilpie •

Fraser Island

Maryborough •

Roma •

Brisbane

Toowoomba •

Warwick •

• Tweed Heads

• Moree

New South Wales

0	300 miles
0	500 km

The world: Whaling

In the past 200 years, global populations of many whale species have been in decline all over the world. This is due to large-scale commercial whaling.

Whales have been hunted from rowing boats for the past 10,000 years by tribes in polar regions, such as the Inuit people. They hunted whales for meat, blubber for fuel, and whalebone for rope. Commercial whaling started during the Industrial Revolution with demand for products such as whale oil to lubricate machines. Whale populations plummeted once explosive harpoons were invented that could kill whales from a distance, and powerful ships could follow whale migrations and process many dead whales.

The humpback whale feeds on krill in polar waters in summer and breeds in tropical waters in winter. Whalers from Russia, USA and Japan hunted during summer in the North Pacific. During the 20th century the global whale population dropped nearly 90 per cent. The International Whaling Commission banned commercial humpback whaling in 1966 to avoid the extinction of the species.

As whales range over such large areas, bans are almost impossible to enforce. Some countries, including Japan, carry on whaling other species for scientific and cultural reasons. Today there are around 60,000 humpbacks and the population is rising, but they still face threats, including pollution and collisions with ships.

N

Greenland

Alaska
(USA)

Canada

NORTH AMERICA

*Pacific
Ocean*

USA

Mexico

Venezuela

SOUTH
AMERICA

Peru

Chile

Argentina

EXPLORE!

Some countries, including Japan and Norway, carry on killing common whales for scientific study, but their shops sell whale meat. Why should these countries follow global bans?

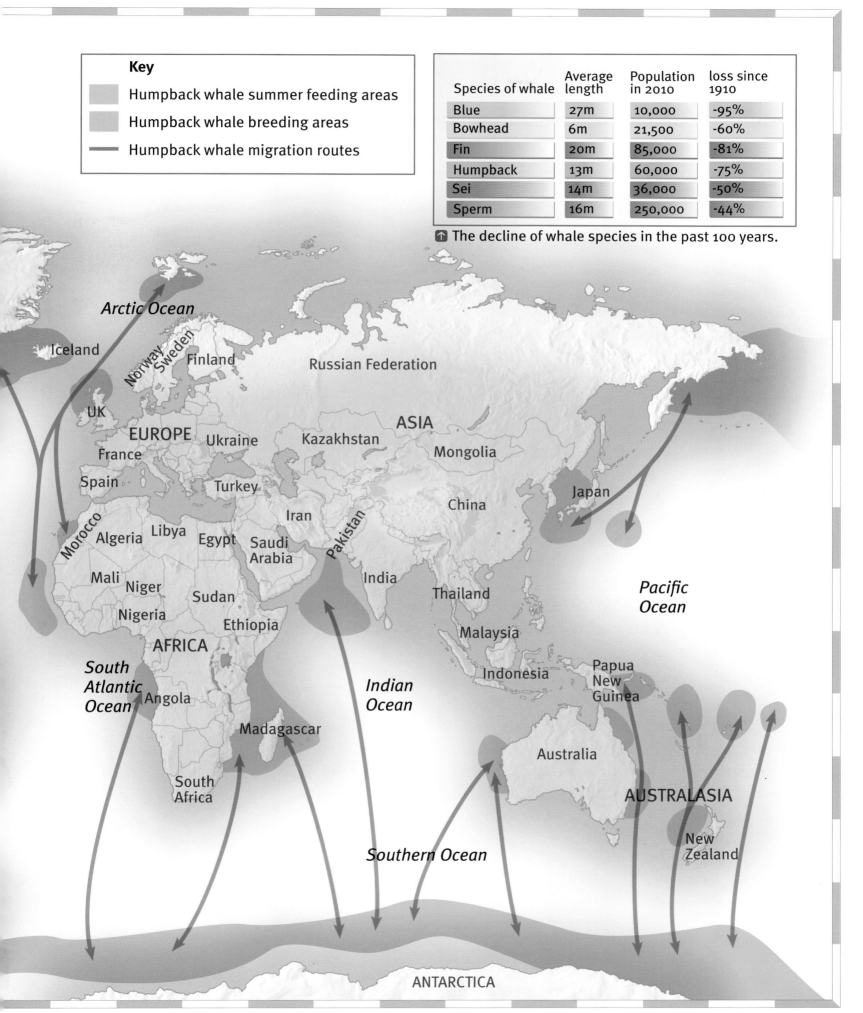

Key

- Humpback whale summer feeding areas
- Humpback whale breeding areas
- Humpback whale migration routes

Species of whale	Average length	Population in 2010	loss since 1910
Blue	27m	10,000	-95%
Bowhead	6m	21,500	-60%
Fin	20m	85,000	-81%
Humpback	13m	60,000	-75%
Sei	14m	36,000	-50%
Sperm	16m	250,000	-44%

↑ The decline of whale species in the past 100 years.

Arctic Ocean

Iceland

Norway Sweden Finland

Russian Federation

UK

EUROPE Ukraine Kazakhstan

ASIA

France

Mongolia

Spain Turkey

Japan

Iran Pakistan

China

Morocco Libya Egypt Saudi Arabia

Algeria

India

Mali Niger Sudan

Thailand

Pacific Ocean

Nigeria Ethiopia

AFRICA

South Atlantic Ocean Angola

Indian Ocean

Malaysia

Papua New Guinea

Indonesia

Madagascar

Australia

South Africa

AUSTRALASIA

New Zealand

Southern Ocean

ANTARCTICA

The world: Overfishing

Fishing is one of the world's most important food industries. It employs about 250 million people globally and supplies around 100 million tonnes of fish per year.

Fish is an important protein source for humans, and as the world population is increasing, so too does the demand for food. The fishing industry is meeting this demand with more efficient fishing boats. They have on-board refrigerators to store the catch and sonar systems to locate fish shoals. However, in certain areas more fish are caught than can be replenished naturally. This is called overfishing.

About 75 per cent of marine fish stocks are now fully exploited or seriously depleted. These include Atlantic cod, Mediterranean/Atlantic tuna and swordfish, and Chilean seabass. Overfishing is sometimes the result of high demand for certain fish. For example, tuna caught globally is in demand from Japan because many people there eat it raw as sushi. The bluefin tuna is now the most endangered fish in the world, mainly due to overfishing. The map shows which other species are being overfished in which areas.

Conservation measures for threatened species include quotas limiting the total weight of fish each boat can catch in a year. They also require the use of large-mesh nets that allow smaller, younger fish to escape, so they may grow and breed. International groups such as the Marine Stewardship Council help conserve threatened fish species by encouraging supermarkets to label fish that where caught sustainably, so consumers can avoid buying overfished species.

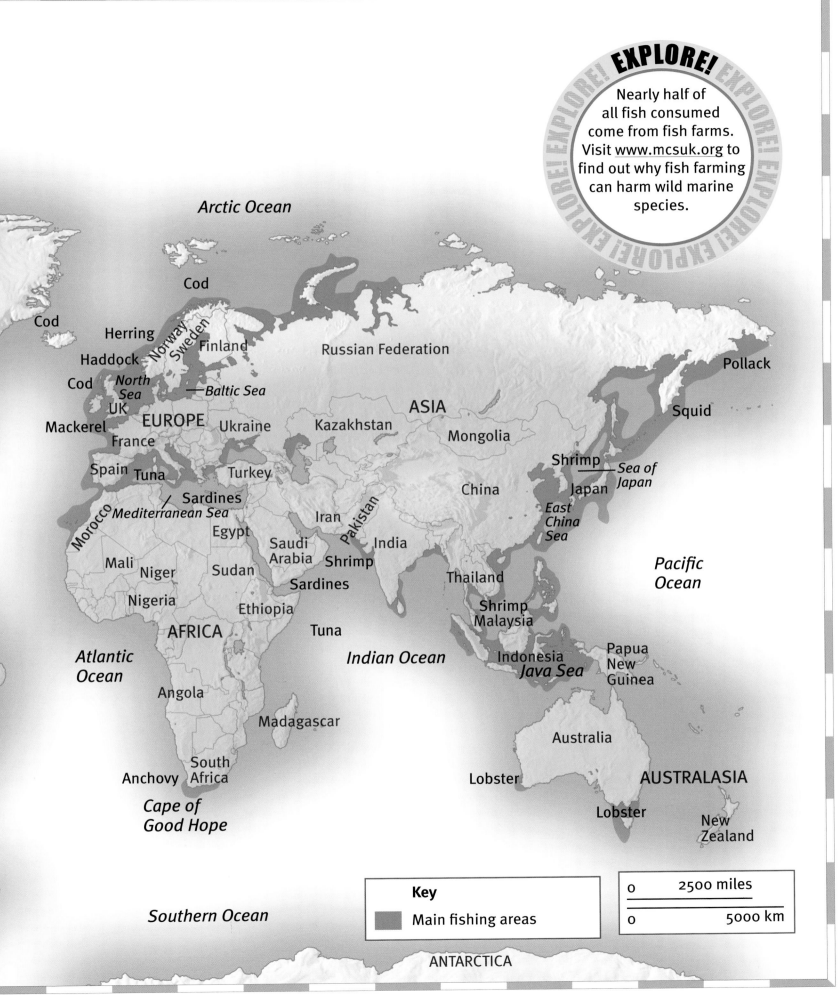

EXPLORE!

Nearly half of all fish consumed come from fish farms. Visit www.mcsuk.org to find out why fish farming can harm wild marine species.

Arctic Ocean

Cod

Cod

Cod

Herring

Haddock

Cod

North Sea

Norway

Sweden

Finland

Baltic Sea

Russian Federation

Pollack

UK

Mackerel

EUROPE

France

Ukraine

Kazakhstan

ASIA

Mongolia

Squid

Spain

Tuna

Turkey

China

Shrimp

Sea of Japan

Japan

Sardines

Mediterranean Sea

Morocco

Egypt

Iran

Pakistan

India

East China Sea

Mali

Niger

Sudan

Saudi Arabia

Shrimp

Sardines

Thailand

Pacific Ocean

Nigeria

Ethiopia

Tuna

Shrimp

Malaysia

AFRICA

Atlantic Ocean

Indian Ocean

Indonesia

Java Sea

Papua New Guinea

Angola

Madagascar

Australia

South Africa

Anchovy

Lobster

AUSTRALASIA

Cape of Good Hope

Lobster

New Zealand

Key

Main fishing areas

0   2500 miles

0   5000 km

Southern Ocean

ANTARCTICA

Europe: Air pollution

Air pollution is when gases and particles make the atmosphere dirty and harm living things. One of the areas where air pollution is very wide-spread is Western Europe.

Most air pollution in Europe is caused by burning fossil fuels in vehicles, power stations and factories to generate energy. This releases gases, such as ozone, and tiny specks of partly burnt fuel. When the gases dissolve in tiny droplets of water, they form acid rain. This rain kills trees because it stops them taking in vital nutrients. It also pollutes lakes, harming freshwater animals, and damages buildings by dissolving stone. Smog is a dangerous form of air pollution made when ozone and tiny specks of burnt fuel (called particulates) react with sunlight. Smog causes breathing problems for people in some cities, including Rome and Moscow.

Across Europe, many cities have Low Emission Zones (LEZs) — areas where heavily polluting vehicles are restricted from entering in order to lower air pollution. For example, from 2008 to 2009, Berlin's diesel particulate levels fell by a quarter after an LEZ was introduced. There are Europe-wide measures to conserve the shared atmosphere. These include limiting harmful emissions from the industry by using special filters or scrubbers in power station chimneys, and encouraging the use of low-emission public transport, such as trams.

⬅ These trees in the Tatra Mountains, Poland, have been badly damaged by air pollution. They have lost almost all their leaves because acid rain has poisoned the soil around them.

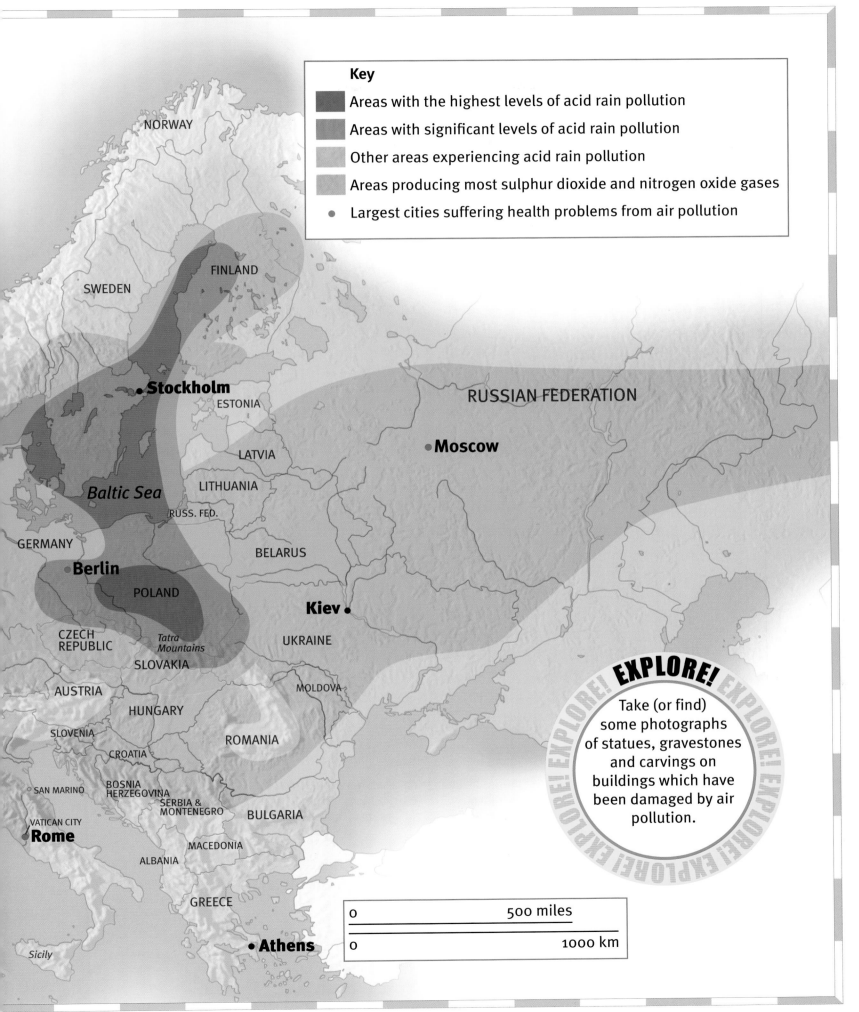

Key

- Areas with the highest levels of acid rain pollution
- Areas with significant levels of acid rain pollution
- Other areas experiencing acid rain pollution
- Areas producing most sulphur dioxide and nitrogen oxide gases
- Largest cities suffering health problems from air pollution

NORWAY

SWEDEN

FINLAND

• **Stockholm**

ESTONIA

Baltic Sea

LATVIA

LITHUANIA

RUSS. FED.

RUSSIAN FEDERATION

• **Moscow**

GERMANY

BELARUS

• **Berlin**

POLAND

CZECH REPUBLIC

Tatra Mountains

Kiev •

SLOVAKIA

UKRAINE

AUSTRIA

MOLDOVA

HUNGARY

SLOVENIA

ROMANIA

CROATIA

• SAN MARINO

BOSNIA HERZEGOVINA

SERBIA & MONTENEGRO

BULGARIA

VATICAN CITY

• **Rome**

MACEDONIA

ALBANIA

GREECE

Sicily

• **Athens**

EXPLORE!

Take (or find) some photographs of statues, gravestones and carvings on buildings which have been damaged by air pollution.

0	500 miles
0	1000 km

The world: Climate change

Climate is the normal pattern of weather in a place throughout the year. When climates change, they have widespread and significant effects on the natural world.

Scientists worldwide are noticing climate changes, including more frequent severe weather events, and warmer, drier or wetter weather than usual every year. Climate change is ultimately caused by global warming. Greenhouse gases in the atmosphere trap heat from the Sun to keep the Earth at a certain temperature. This is called the greenhouse effect. However, burning fuels and other human activities adds more greenhouse gas, including carbon dioxide, to the atmosphere. This increases the greenhouse effect and causes global warming. Higher temperatures in some areas evaporate more water causing increased rain, or creating stronger winds. Sea levels are gradually rising because glaciers are melting. Warm seawater also takes up more space than cold seawater.

The map shows some of the effects of climate change worldwide. With continued global warming, scientists predict that many coastal settlements could become submerged. Already, some Pacific islands have been abandoned for this reason. People are trying to slow climate change by using solar and wind power, for example, rather than burning fossils fuels for energy. They are also adapting to climate change, for example by building hurricane-proof housing and flood defences.

NORTH AMERICA

Atlantic Ocean

SOUTH AMERICA

Key: The effects of climate change

Extreme heat/drought
1 European heatwave 2003: 35,000 die in countries including France, Italy and Netherlands
2 African drought 2006: 17 million face food shortages in the Horn of Africa
3 Indonesian fires 1998: worst forest fires ever; 70 million people have health problems due to inhaling smoke

Extreme rain/wind
4 Pakistan floods 2010: 8 million people are homeless and 1,750 die
5 China landslides 2010: millions of people are affected when heavy rains cause landslides
6 Brazil hurricane 2004: the first ever recorded in the South Atlantic

Rising temperatures
7 Siberian permafrost: a 3 °C rise is turning frozen land to new lakes and making houses subside
8 Canadian polar bears: with less sea ice to catch seals, bear numbers reduce and cause them to find food in towns

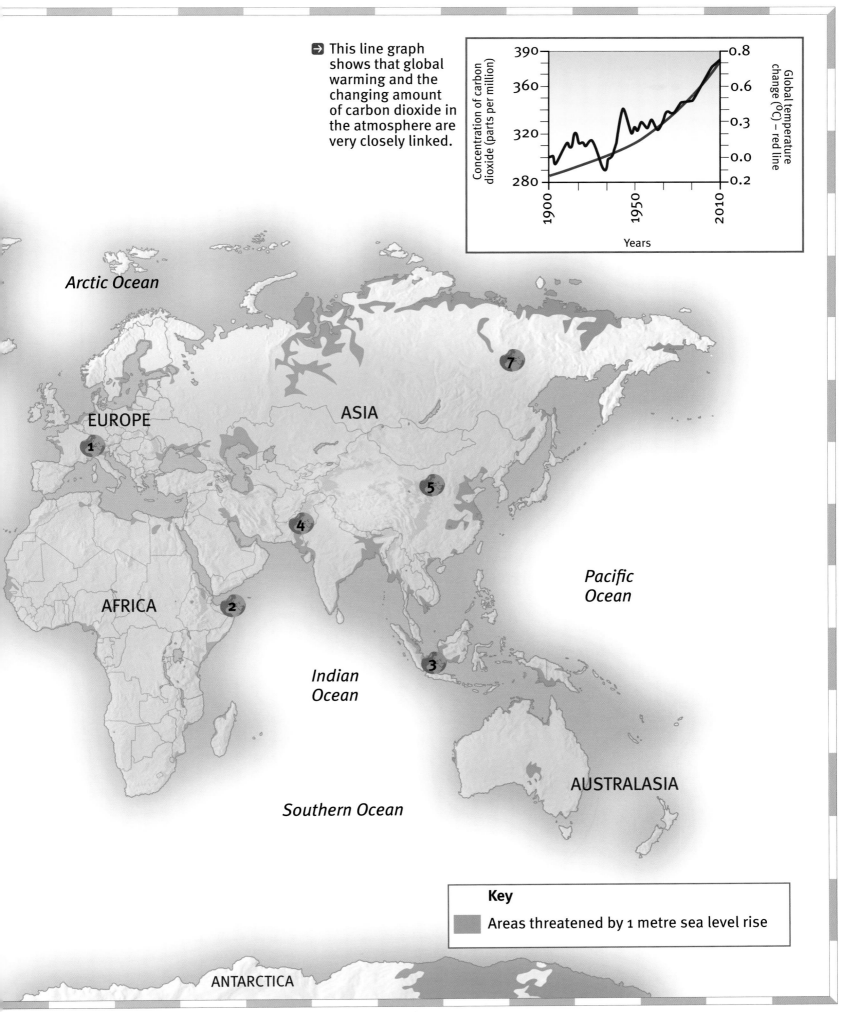

➡ This line graph shows that global warming and the changing amount of carbon dioxide in the atmosphere are very closely linked.

Concentration of carbon dioxide (parts per million)

Global temperature change ($^{\circ}$C) – red line

390
360
320
280

0.8
0.6
0.3
0.0
-0.2

1900   1950   2010

Years

Arctic Ocean

EUROPE

ASIA

AFRICA

Pacific Ocean

Indian Ocean

Southern Ocean

AUSTRALASIA

Key

Areas threatened by 1 metre sea level rise

ANTARCTICA

Now test yourself!

These questions will help you to revisit some of the information in this book. To answer the questions, you will need to use the contents on page 2 and the index on page 32, as well as the relevant pages on each topic.

1 Use the contents on page 2 to find which pages show a map of:

(a) the forests in South America.

(b) wetland conservation in Europe.

(c) seas and oceans that have been overfished.

2 Use the index on page 32 to find the pages which will tell you:

(a) which gases make up the Earth's atmosphere.

(b) which country the Everglades National Park is in.

3 Use pages 10–11 to find out which animal produces ivory and what this valuable material is made into.

4 Use pages 14–15 to name the wetland in southern France which is famous for its horses and flamingos.

5 Use pages 20–21 to find out how damage to coral reefs can be caused by:

(a) changes in the natural environment.

(b) the activities of people.

6 Name the natural features shown on this map by these letters: desert A, island B, rainforest C, marine feature D, fishing area E.

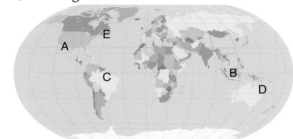

7 Use different pages in the book to pair these species with their correct natural habitats:

species: buffalo, crocodile, giant panda, lichen, polyps.

habitats: bamboo forest, bare rock face, coral reef, freshwater lake, grassland.

8 What are the main conservation reasons for having:

(a) armed gamekeepers?

(b) Clean Air Acts?

(c) fishing quotas?

(d) Sites of Special Scientific Interest?

Glossary

climate change any long-term significant changes to the weather pattern of a certain area. Climate change can have natural causes, such as volcano eruptions, and is also the result of global warming.

conservation the care of species and environments to ensure their survival for future generations.

coral underwater reefs made up of limestone skeleton deposited by polyps.

deforestation the loss of forest due to felling large numbers of trees.

desertification the word used to describe the spread of the world's deserts.

drought a long period of time with much less rainfall than usual.

ecosystem a part of the natural world, including the animals and plants living in it.

environment the natural environment is made up of hills, rivers, lakes and wildlife; the human environment includes buildings and roads.

erosion the wearing away of the land surface by wind and water.

extinction what happens when the very last member of a species dies.

global warming rising temperatures worldwide, caused by the increase of gases in the air that trap the Sun's heat near the Earth.

greenhouse effect the warming effect on the atmosphere of burning fossil fuels; this is one cause of global warming.

heritage valuable human and natural features inherited from the past.

irrigation to water farming land.

migration the seasonal movement of wildlife in search of food throughout the year.

National Park large area where the scenery is so attractive that strict rules protect it.

pollution damage to the environment caused by harmful substances.

species a group of plants or a kind of wildlife which has the same features.

wetlands areas where soil is permanently saturated with water.

Index

First published in 2011 by Wayland
Copyright © Wayland 2011

Wayland
Hachette Children's Books
338 Euston Road
London NW1 3BH

Wayland Australia
Level 17/207
Kent Street
Sydney, NSW 2000

Editor: Julia Adams
Designer: Rob Walster, Big Blu Design
Cover design: Wayland
Map Art: Martin Sanders
Illustrations: Andy Stagg
Picture research: Kathy Lockley/ Julia Adams

The website addresses (URLs) included in this book
were valid at the time of going to press. However, it is
possible that contents or addresses may have changed
since the publication of this book No responsibility for
any such changes can be accepted by either the author
or the Publisher.

British Library Cataloguing in Publication Data
Gillett, Jack.
  Maps of the environmental world.
  Conservation areas.
  1. Natural resources conservation areas--Juvenile
  literature. 2. Natural resources conservation areas--Maps
  for children.
  I. Title II. Gillett, Meg.
  333.9'516-dc22

ISBN 978 0 7502 6240 8

Printed in Malaysia

Wayland is a division of Hachette Children's Books,
an Hachette UK company.
www.hachette.co.uk

Picture acknowledgements:
All photography: Shutterstock, except: p. 8: Edwin
Remsberg/Alamy; p. 17, p. 18 (right): iStock Images;
p. 18 (left): NASA/Goddard Space Flight Center Scientific
Visualization Studio.

Maps of the Environmental World

Contents of titles in the series:

WAYLAND